Seven Wonders of
MEDICINE

Karen Gunnison Ballen

TWENTY-FIRST CENTURY BOOKS

Minneapolis

To Bear, with love

I thank Dr. Jan P. Hessler for his helpful comments on nanomedicine and Peg Goldstein for her editorial guidance. And a special thanks to Dr. Fred Bortz, who introduced me to the joy of writing about science for kids.

Twenty-First Century Books
A division of Lerner Publishing Group, Inc.
241 First Avenue North
Minneapolis, MN 55401 U.S.A.

Website address: www.lernerbooks.com

Library of Congress Cataloging-in-Publication Data

Ballen, Karen Gunnison.
    Seven wonders of medicine / by Karen Gunnison Ballen.
        p.   cm.
    Includes bibliographical references and index.
    ISBN 978–0–7613–4239–7 (lib. bdg. : alk. paper)
    1. Medical innovations—Juvenile literature. I. Title.
RA418.5.M4B35 2010
610—dc22   2009020316

Manufactured in the United States of America
1 – DP – 12/15/09

Contents

INTRODUCTION

*P*EOPLE LOVE TO MAKE LISTS OF THE BIGGEST AND THE BEST. ALMOST TWENTY-FIVE HUNDRED YEARS AGO, A GREEK WRITER NAMED HERODOTUS MADE A LIST OF THE MOST AWESOME THINGS EVER BUILT BY PEOPLE. THE LIST INCLUDED BUILDINGS, STATUES, AND OTHER OBJECTS THAT WERE LARGE, WONDROUS, AND IMPRESSIVE. LATER, OTHER WRITERS ADDED NEW ITEMS TO THE LIST. WRITERS EVENTUALLY AGREED ON A FINAL LIST. IT WAS CALLED THE SEVEN WONDERS OF THE ANCIENT WORLD.

The list became so famous that people began imitating it. They made other lists of wonders. They listed the Seven Wonders of the Modern World. They listed the Seven Wonders of Nature, including mountains, canyons, and other natural formations. This book is about the Seven Wonders of Medicine. These wonders are not large objects such as buildings or mountains. These wonders are ideas, tools, and discoveries.

MEDICINE IN HISTORY

Medicine is the art and science of healing. People have studied and practiced medicine for thousands of years. In ancient times, doctors wrote about diseases and how to treat them. But those doctors did not know much about how the human body worked. They did not know how diseases spread.

The study of medicine has changed a great deal since then. Our ideas about disease have changed too. In modern times, we know that germs cause disease. We know that keeping streets clean and washing our hands can help keep germs from spreading. We also know about vaccines—the injections that can protect us from certain diseases. Modern doctors can cure many illnesses with medicine or surgery. Many important discoveries and inventions made modern medicine possible.

A Wondrous Journey

You are about to go on a journey of discovery. The first stop is Europe in the 1600s. You will see how the first microscopes opened a new world to the scientists there. Next, you'll learn about the discovery of vaccination. This tool allowed doctors to prevent one of the most dreaded diseases in human history. You'll also find out how insulin, antibiotics, and new surgical techniques saved millions of lives in the twentieth century.

The last stop on our journey is the twenty-first century, where modern scientists are discovering new ways to find, treat, and cure diseases. Modern doctors can even replace body parts that do not work properly. To find out more, turn the page and begin your journey of discovery.

Above: *Vaccinations are often given with a syringe.* **Right:** *Microscopes like this one opened up a world to doctors and scientists.*

1 Microscopy

This image, made with an electron microscope, shows the Epstein-Barr virus. Microscopes enable doctors and scientists to see disease-causing organisms such as viruses.

*I*N EARLIER CENTURIES, MEDICAL KNOWLEDGE WAS VERY LIMITED. EVEN DOCTORS DID NOT KNOW MUCH ABOUT THE HUMAN BODY AND HOW IT WORKS. NO ONE KNEW THAT ALL LIVING THINGS ARE MADE OF TINY UNITS CALLED CELLS. NO ONE KNEW ABOUT TINY LIVING THINGS THAT ARE MUCH TOO SMALL FOR HUMANS TO SEE.

Many people died of communicable diseases. These diseases can pass from one person to another. The flu is a communicable disease. The virus that causes flu can pass from one student in your class to another. Hundreds of years ago, no one knew what caused the flu and other diseases. Some people, including many doctors, thought that poisons in the air caused diseases. Others thought that diseases were a punishment from God.

This fourteenth-century European illustration shows surgeons operating on a wounded soldier.

In modern times, these ideas might seem strange or even silly. But we have to remember that germs—living things that can cause disease—are too small to be seen with the eyes alone. Doctors in earlier eras did not know what caused disease because they did not know about germs. To learn about germs, people needed to see them.

LARGER THAN LIFE

Put a pencil in a glass of water. Notice that the part of the pencil in the water looks bigger than the portion that's out of the water. Water bends light rays, making objects look closer than they really are. Because the objects look closer, they also look larger.

Lenses also bend light rays. Lenses are curved pieces of glass or other clear substances. Concave lenses—which are thicker at the edges than at the center—make things look smaller. Convex lenses—which are thicker at the center than at the edges—make things look bigger.

Humans and other animals have lenses in their eyes. The lenses bend light rays entering our eyes. Lenses help us see objects clearly. They help us see objects that are close as well as far away.

HIGHER *Power*

How do you make a more powerful lens? The magnifying power of a lens depends on how curved it is. A lens that has a sharp curve will magnify an image more than a lens with a gentle curve.

This magnifying glass is a convex lens. Objects viewed through a convex lens look bigger.

"Where the telescope ends, the microscope begins."
—*French author Victor Hugo*, Les Misérables, *1862*

SEEING UP CLOSE . . . *and Far Away*

Around the same time people invented microscopes, they also invented telescopes *(below, from the seventeenth century)*. Telescopes and microscopes both use lenses to bend light rays. But they use different kinds of lenses. Telescopes make objects that are far away look close. Microscopes make objects that are close look bigger.

THE FIRST MICROSCOPES

In the Middle Ages (about A.D. 500 to 1500), people in Europe began to learn about lenses. By the 900s, they knew how to make convex lenses. An unknown European inventor created the first eyeglasses in the 1200s.

The people who made eyeglasses worked with different kinds of lenses. Eventually, someone looked through two convex lenses at once. The two lenses together magnified (enlarged) images much more than one lens alone.

Around 1590 two Dutch eyeglass makers built a tube with glass lenses at each end. This device made objects look about nine times bigger than they really were. It allowed the eyeglass makers to see things that were normally too small to be seen. A device that magnifies tiny objects is called a microscope.

EARLY MICROSCOPE MASTERS

Robert Hooke, an English scientist of the 1600s, was curious about many things in nature. He wanted to see the details of nature clearly. He wanted to study tiny insects and animal parts, such as the wings of flies.

Microscopy

9

Hooke looked at objects through a magnifying glass. But it was not powerful enough. So he built a microscope that magnified images about twenty-five times. The microscope let him see tiny spaces in a piece of cork. The spaces reminded him of cells, or small rooms. So he called them cells.

Hooke looked at many things under his microscope. He drew pictures of fleas, sea animals, and fossils as he saw them under his microscope. In 1665 Hooke wrote a book called *Micrographia*. The book included Hooke's drawings.

A Dutch cloth merchant named Antoni van Leeuwenhoek also used microscopes. He used them to count threads in the cloth that he sold. After Leeuwenhoek read Hooke's book, he wanted to look at living things under a microscope too. He began to work with lenses.

Leeuwenhoek made many small, handheld microscopes. These were by far the best microscopes of the time. One of his microscopes magnified things to 270 times their real size. Leeuwenhoek could see things that no one else could see.

Leeuwenhoek wondered why spices such as pepper have such a strong taste. In 1674 he soaked pepper in water. After three weeks, Leeuwenhoek looked at the pepper water under his microscope. He saw that tiny organisms from the air and the pepper had started to grow in the water. Leeuwenhoek called the tiny organisms animalcules. The word means "little animals."

Leeuwenhoek wanted to see more animalcules. He scraped plaque off people's teeth. He found many tiny organisms in those samples.

Scientist Robert Hooke used a microscope like this one in the 1660s.

Robert Hooke created drawings of many of the items he looked at through his microscope. These items included an ant (above) and cork tissue (below). Hooke put the images in his book Micrographia (right).

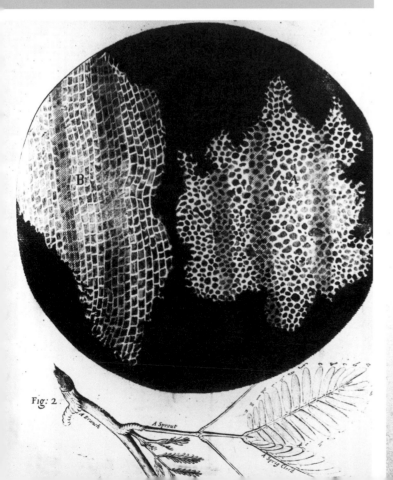

Fig: 2

A Branch   A Sprout   A Sprig Clo'd

MICROGRAPHIA:

OR SOME
Physiological Descriptions

OF

MINUTE BODIES

MADE BY

MAGNIFYING GLASSES.

WITH

OBSERVATIONS and INQUIRIES thereupon.

By *R. HOOKE*, Fellow of the ROYAL SOCIETY.

Non poſsis oculo quantum contendere Linceus,
Non tamen idcirco contemnas Lippus inungi. Horat. Ep. Lib. 1.

LONDON, Printed for *John Martyn*, Printer to the ROYAL SOCIETY, and are to be ſold at his Shop at the *Bell* a little without *Temple Barr.* MDCLXVII.

Leeuwenhoek also found tiny organisms in pond water. He looked at drops of blood under his microscope and became the first person to see red blood cells. He also watched maggots, fleas, and lice hatch from tiny eggs. Leeuwenhoek wrote about his discoveries so that other scientists could read about them.

Leeuwenhoek showed that we are surrounded by a world of tiny creatures. He did not know that some of these creatures cause disease. No one did.

In the 1800s, scientists learned to build more powerful lenses. They used the lenses to make more powerful microscopes and new discoveries.

This seventeenth-century portrait shows Antoni van Leeuwenhoek. Leeuwenhoek built the most powerful microscopes of his era.

GERMS CAUSE DISEASE

Bacteria are tiny, one-celled creatures. In the late 1800s, some scientists wondered whether bacteria could cause disease. But most scientists didn't think so. They still thought that poisons in the air caused disease.

Robert Koch, a German scientist, used his microscope to learn about bacteria and disease. Koch used a microscope to look at blood from cattle that had a disease called anthrax. He saw some bacteria in the blood. He found the same bacteria in the blood of other cattle that suffered from anthrax. But Koch did not see the bacteria in the blood of healthy animals. This observation helped Koch prove that the bacteria caused anthrax. He did a

"I found an unbelievably great company of living animalcules, a-swimming more nimbly than any I had ever seen up to this time."

—Antoni van Leeuwenhoek, 1683

THE SMALLEST *Units of Life*

Cells are tiny units that make up living things. Every cell has a covering that separates it from everything around it. Every cell contains material called deoxyribonucleic acid (DNA). DNA holds the instructions that cells need to survive, grow, and reproduce. Humans are made of trillions of cells. Some organisms are made of only one cell.

similar experiment with a disease called tuberculosis. With these experiments, he was able to prove that germs, not poisons in the air, cause disease.

MICROSCOPES IN SURGERY

One hundred years ago, doctors had a hard time performing some kinds of surgery. They couldn't see humans' tiny nerves, blood vessels, and other body parts. Many doctors used magnifying glasses to help them. But they needed something stronger.

In 1921 a Swedish ear surgeon named Carl Nylen built a surgical microscope. This device helped him perform delicate operations on tiny parts of the human ear. Later, doctors used microscopes for other types of surgery. Microscopes made new types of surgery possible.

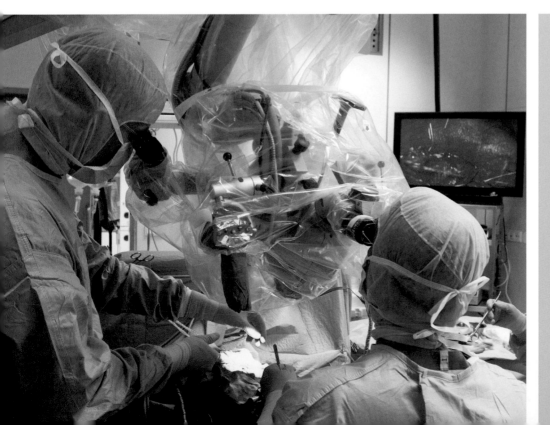

This neurosurgical team uses a microscope during a brain operation.

MORE POWERFUL MICROSCOPES

The first microscopes were called optical microscopes. They used lenses to bend light rays. The most powerful optical microscopes can magnify objects about two thousand times. They allow people to see tiny objects such as bacteria. To see things smaller than bacteria, such as viruses and the structures inside cells, scientists needed a different kind of microscope.

In 1931 German scientists Ernst Ruska and Max Knoll built an electron microscope. Electron microscopes use tiny particles called electrons to magnify images. Modern electron microscopes can magnify images up to two million times. They allow people to see inside cells. With electron microscopes, scientists can study the shape and structure of viruses. They can magnify human tissue to look for tumors and disease.

Scientists Gerd Binnig and Heinrich Rohrer invented the scanning tunneling microscope in 1981. This microscope allows scientists to see atoms, the basic units of matter. An atom is more than a million times smaller than the thickness of a human hair. The scanning tunneling microscope uses electrical signals to make maps of the surface of atoms and other objects. The microscope allows doctors and scientists to see inside cells. This work helps doctors diagnose, or recognize, diseases.

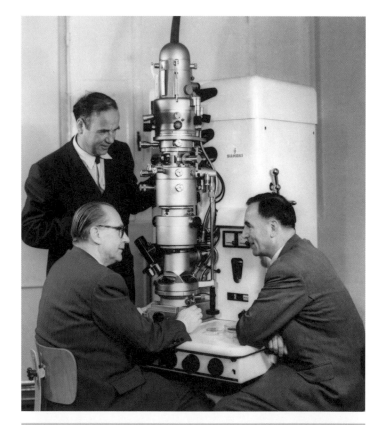

Scientists invented the atomic force microscope in 1986. This device is similar to the scanning tunneling microscope. It even allows scientists to move atoms around.

Microscopes have come a long way since Hooke discovered cells and Leeuwenhoek watched lice hatch. These early masters opened a new world to all of us.

Ernst Ruska (right) *and two other researchers pose with an electron microscope in the early 1940s.*

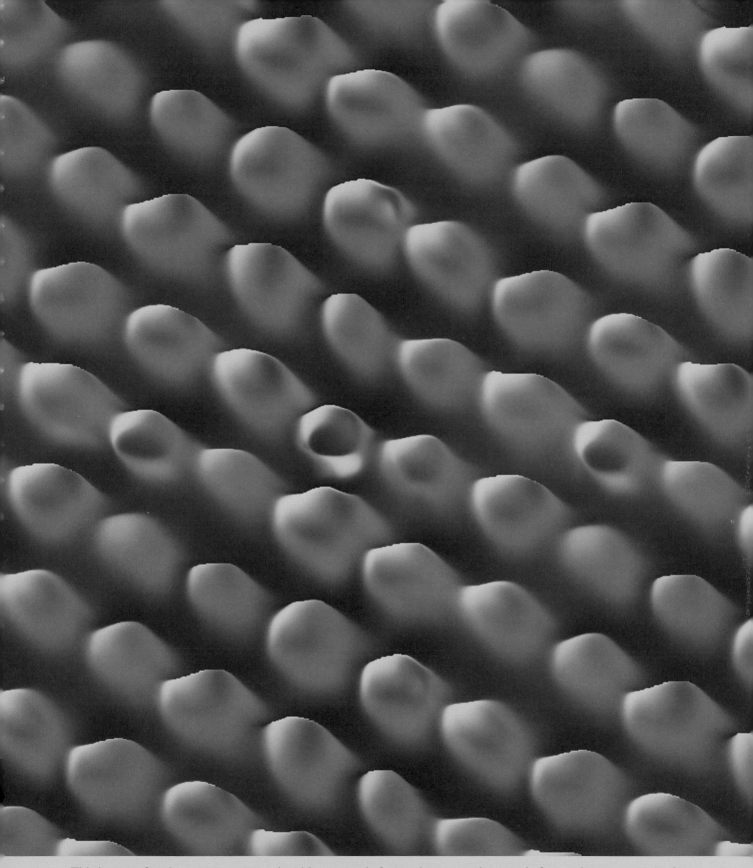

This image of carbon atoms was made with an atomic force microscope. An atomic force microscope maps the surface of atoms to create an image. The color is added later.

2 Vaccination

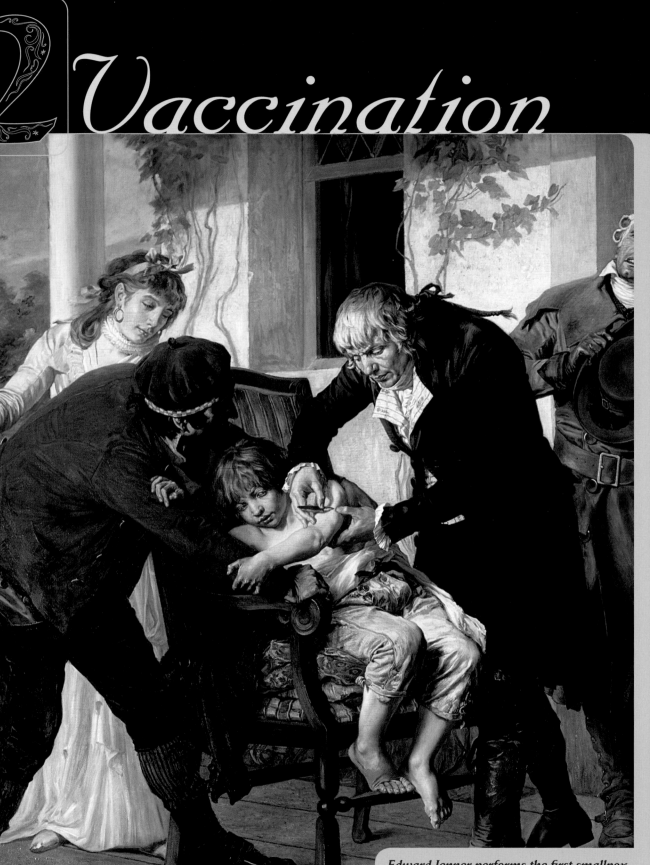

Edward Jenner performs the first smallpox vaccination in Britain in 1796. This French painting of the event was created in 1879.

*T*HE HUMAN IMMUNE SYSTEM IS A NETWORK OF CELLS AND ORGANS THAT KEEP PEOPLE HEALTHY. WHEN YOUR IMMUNE SYSTEM FIGHTS A GERM, IT MAKES SUBSTANCES CALLED ANTIBODIES. ANTIBODIES HELP DESTROY GERMS.

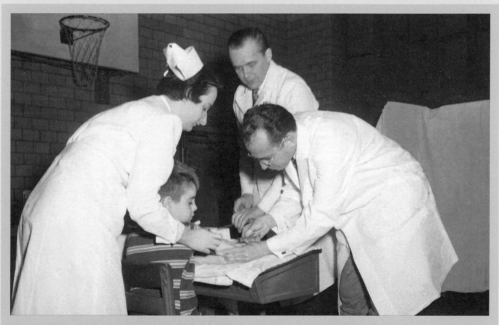

Jonas Salk (right) *administers the polio vaccine to a boy in the 1950s. Such vaccinations have saved millions of lives.*

For example, if you get sick with the measles, your immune system will make antibodies to the measles virus. The next time the virus tries to attack you, your immune system will make measles antibodies extremely fast—before you even get sick. In this way, your immune system keeps you from getting some diseases more than once.

Hundreds of years ago, doctors did not know about the immune system. They did not know why people who got certain diseases, such as the measles, never got the same diseases again.

CATCHING SMALLPOX ON PURPOSE?

Smallpox is an especially deadly disease. It is named for the small, pus-filled sores it makes on the skin of people who suffer from it. These sores are called pustules or pocks. Smallpox has been around for thousands of years. It once affected people in most of the world. In the late 1700s, smallpox killed up to four hundred thousand Europeans each year. Some people survived the disease, but it left them blind or badly scarred. People needed a way to protect themselves from this dreaded disease.

People in Africa, China, India, and the Middle East fought smallpox with a practice called variolation. Variolation involved giving someone smallpox on purpose. People who were variolated caught a very mild case of smallpox, which usually didn't kill them. After a person had smallpox, he or she wouldn't get the disease again. In China people variolated themselves by inhaling powdered crusts of smallpox pustules. In Persia (modern-day Iran), people variolated themselves by swallowing powdered crusts. In Turkey and other countries, doctors took the thick liquid from smallpox pustules and rubbed it into scratches on the arms of healthy people.

THE ADAMS Family

In 1764 future U.S. president John Adams underwent variolation for smallpox during an epidemic in colonial America. During an epidemic in 1776, Adam's wife, Abigail, had herself and her four children variolated. Variolation made all the Adamses sick with smallpox, but the disease did not kill any of them. Variolation also kept the family from getting smallpox during later epidemics.

Doctors in Great Britain did not believe that variolation was effective. They didn't want to test the practice because smallpox was so deadly. If a doctor accidentally killed a patient with smallpox, no one would trust the doctor again.

But in the early 1700s, a British woman visited Turkey. She saw that variolation worked well there. She had her children variolated in Great Britain to show others that the practice was safe and effective.

British doctors began to use the procedure. They used pus from people with mild cases of smallpox. They rubbed the pus into cuts on the arms of healthy people. After several days, a patient usually came down with a mild case of smallpox. After that, the patient never caught smallpox again.

Variolation was not completely safe. Some variolated people got severe cases of smallpox instead of mild ones. Sometimes, healthy people who hadn't been variolated caught severe smallpox from variolated people. But many more people died of natural smallpox than of variolation. Even so, some countries outlawed variolation. Other countries made strict rules about how variolation could be done.

This photograph, taken in 1974, shows a Bengali boy with smallpox.

THE COWPOX CONNECTION

A British doctor named Edward Jenner was variolated as a child. He got a bad case of smallpox and almost died. He wanted to find a safer way to protect people from smallpox.

Cowpox is a mild disease that mostly affects cows. In Great Britain in the 1700s, people who milked cows often caught the disease. But cowpox was not serious. No one died from it. After someone had cowpox, he or she did not catch smallpox, even during smallpox epidemics (outbreaks). Many people thought that having cowpox protected them from smallpox. But most doctors did not agree. They thought the idea was an old wives' tale, or superstition.

Jenner heard about the cowpox connection from a woman who milked cows. He learned that some farmers infected themselves with pus from cows that had cowpox. Jenner decided to study cowpox and smallpox.

In 1796 Jenner was ready to experiment. He took pus from a cowpox pustule on the hand of a woman named Sarah Nelmes. He rubbed the pus into cuts on the arm of a boy named James Phipps. Phipps soon came down with cowpox. When Jenner variolated him several weeks later, Phipps did not catch smallpox. In this way, Jenner proved that an infection with cowpox can protect

BATTLING SMALLPOX IN THE *New World*

In the late 1700s, King Charles IV of Spain wanted to send the cowpox virus to Spain's colonies in the Americas and the Philippines. He wanted to use the virus to vaccinate people against smallpox. But people then didn't know how to transport the cowpox virus without it going bad.

A doctor named Francisco de Balmis had an idea. In 1803 he left Spain on a ship with twenty-two orphan boys. During the voyage, Balmis vaccinated the boys, two at a time, every ten days. After a boy was vaccinated, he developed cowpox. Balmis then transferred the cowpox from that boy to another. In this way, Balmis always had cowpox virus available. At ports along the way, he vaccinated local people. Other doctors then carried the vaccine farther and in different directions. Doctors vaccinated more than one hundred thousand people in Spanish colonies this way.

> *"The annihilation [destruction] of smallpox—the most dreadful scourge of the human race—will be the final result of this practice [vaccination]."*
>
> —Edward Jenner, 1801

people from smallpox. Since the Latin word for "cow" is *vacca*, Jenner called his procedure vaccination.

Jenner was not the first person to use cowpox as a smallpox vaccination. But he was the one who proved to doctors that it was safe and effective. Jenner had changed vaccination from an old wives' tale into a scientifically tested medical tool.

COWPOX POISON

Many people in Europe did not like vaccination. They didn't think that doctors should give people a disease from animals. They said that vaccinations were "cowpox poison." Some artists drew cartoons of vaccinated people with bulls' horns growing from their heads.

This cartoon from 1802 expresses the fears some people had about the cowpox vaccine.

Vaccination caused another problem. Sometimes, when doctors took cowpox pus from one person and gave it to another person, a different disease was passed along with cowpox.

But vaccination was still pretty safe. Over time, more people accepted the idea of vaccination. Parents had their children vaccinated. Soon smallpox outbreaks happened less often.

In modern times, we know that cowpox and smallpox viruses are very similar. When someone is vaccinated, his or her immune system makes antibodies that can fight both the cowpox virus and the smallpox virus. If the smallpox virus tries to attack a vaccinated person, the antibodies will destroy the virus before the person becomes sick.

THE SEARCH FOR MORE VACCINES

Many more diseases, such as cholera, tuberculosis, and whooping cough, made people very sick and sometimes killed them. Unlike smallpox, these diseases did not have a milder form that could be used for vaccination. Doctors needed other ways to protect people from disease.

In the late 1800s, French scientist

WHAT HAPPENED *to Smallpox?*

In 1967 the World Health Organization made a plan to get rid of smallpox on Earth. Doctors vaccinated people all over the world. If someone did get smallpox, he or she had to stay away from healthy people. By the end of 1979, smallpox was completely gone. No one anywhere in the world had the disease. So no one could pass it to anyone else. Since smallpox is gone, kids don't need to be vaccinated against smallpox anymore.

Louis Pasteur experiments with vaccines.

> *"Immunization is a proven tool for controlling and eliminating life-threatening infectious diseases and is estimated to avert [prevent] over two million deaths each year."*
>
> —*World Health Organization, 2009*

Louis Pasteur made vaccines against cholera, anthrax, and rabies. Pasteur made his vaccines by weakening germs that caused these diseases. The weakened germs made people only slightly sick. The germs also triggered the immune system to make antibodies to fight the diseases. In that way, the vaccines protected people from getting the diseases in the future.

In modern times, doctors give vaccinations to babies and young children. The vaccinations protect children from many serious illnesses, such as polio, whooping cough, mumps, and measles. By vaccinating children, doctors have wiped out polio in many places. Whooping cough, mumps, and measles have become rare. (Some people who have not been vaccinated still catch these diseases.) We have come a long way since the days when many people of all ages died from these diseases.

HOW DO THEY *Know That?*

How did Louis Pasteur realize that weakened germs can be used as vaccines? He told his assistant to inject chickens with bacteria that cause cholera. But his assistant went on vacation without doing it. When the assistant returned, he injected the chickens with the bacteria. By then the bacteria were very old and weak. The bacteria did not kill the chickens. Instead, the chickens just became a little sick. Pasteur injected the chickens again, this time with fresh bacteria. This time the chickens didn't get sick at all. The weakened bacteria from the first injections had protected them from cholera.

3 Insulin

This image shows manufactured insulin at 160 times magnification. Insulin has greatly improved life expectancy and quality of life for diabetics.

*J*N EARLIER CENTURIES, A CHILD WHO GOT DIABETES WOULD LIVE FOR ONLY A FEW YEARS. THE CHILD WOULD DIE BECAUSE HIS OR HER BODY COULD NOT USE FOOD TO MAKE ENERGY.

U.S. Supreme Court justice Sonia Sotomayor was diagnosed with type I diabetes when she was eight years old.

A person with diabetes has a pancreas that does not work properly. The pancreas is an organ that makes a substance called insulin. Insulin helps the body turn sugar from food into energy.

Glucose is a kind of sugar. People with untreated diabetes have too much glucose in their blood. Diabetics (people with diabetes) urinate often to get rid of the extra glucose. They are always thirsty because they lose so much water in their urine. They are also always hungry because their bodies don't use glucose properly to make energy. Untreated diabetes leads to many serious health problems. Without treatment, diabetics get terribly thin and soon die.

Modern doctors use insulin to treat diabetes. With insulin, diabetics can live long and healthy lives. The discovery of insulin was a great breakthrough in medicine.

HISTORY OF "THE SWEET FLOW"

In ancient times, diabetes was sometimes called the sweet flow, because the urine of diabetics contained so much sugar. Doctors thought that urine was the key to diabetes. Some doctors thought that diabetics had problems with their kidneys, the organs that make urine. Others thought that the bladder was the problem. The bladder is the organ that stores urine.

In 1889 German doctors Oskar Minkowski and Joseph von Mering wondered what the organ called the pancreas did. They removed the pancreas

Oskar Minkowski (near right) *and Joseph von Mering* (far right) *discovered that the pancreas was linked to diabetes.*

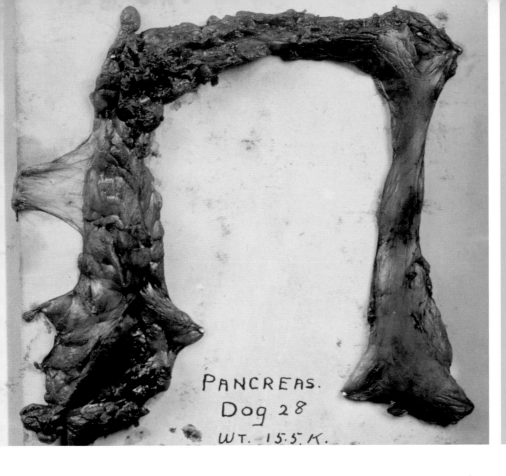

This is a dog pancreas. In the 1800s, scientists discovered the link between the pancreas and diabetes by removing a dog's pancreas and observing the effects.

from a dog to see what would happen. Mering left on vacation. But Minkowski was able to watch the dog.

The dog started drinking much more water. He urinated on the floor of the laboratory, even though he was housebroken. He urinated much more often than he did before his pancreas was removed. Minkowski tested the dog's urine. He found a lot of glucose in it. Then Minkowski tested the dog's blood. It also contained more glucose than it should have. The dog had become diabetic. But why?

Minkowski put a piece of a pancreas under the skin of the diabetic dog. The dog stopped drinking and urinating so much. He started again when the piece of pancreas was removed. Minkowski realized that the pancreas made a substance that helped the body use glucose to make energy.

THE SEARCH FOR INSULIN

Scientists began looking for this substance in the pancreases of animals. They called the substance insulin. But the scientists didn't know much about insulin. That made finding it very difficult.

These four men were instrumental in finding and producing insulin to treat diabetics. Above: *John Macleod in the late 1920s. Right: James Collip works in a laboratory in the late 1920s. Below: Frederick Banting (left) and Charles Best (right) stand outside of a research lab in Toronto, Canada.*

Four scientists—John Macleod, Frederick Banting, Charles Best, and James Collip—worked together in Canada. In 1921 they were able to get insulin from the pancreases of cows. Doctors could use this insulin to treat human diabetics.

Leonard Thompson was a fourteen-year-old boy with diabetes. He was expected to die soon. In January 1922, Thompson became the first diabetic to be treated with insulin. After a few months of insulin shots, Thompson was healthy.

But doctors needed a lot of insulin to treat all diabetics. They were frustrated. They knew that insulin would save the lives of many people. But they just couldn't figure out how to make enough of it.

During this time, doctors kept their diabetic patients on strict diets. The diets helped control the amount of glucose in patients' blood. The doctors hoped to keep their patients alive until more insulin was available. More scientists went to work and learned how to make large amounts of insulin from animal pancreases. After that, doctors could treat many diabetics.

INSULIN IN ACTION

Elizabeth Hughes was diagnosed with diabetes when she was eleven. Her doctor put her on a very strict diet. Hughes wasn't allowed to eat bread or sweets. Some days she couldn't eat at all. On days that she could eat, she had to weigh every bit of

"To think that I'll be leading a normal, healthy existence is beyond all comprehension." "Oh, [insulin] is simply too wonderful for words."
—*Diabetic Elizabeth Hughes, 1922*

food to make sure she didn't eat too much. She was miserable on such a strict diet. But she followed it carefully.

In August 1922, Hughes traveled to Toronto, Canada, for insulin shots. She received her first shot three days before her fifteenth birthday. By then she weighed only 45 pounds (20 kilograms). She could barely walk. The insulin made her feel better right away. Soon she was able to eat a normal diet, as long as she took insulin several times a day. She lived to the age of seventy-three in good health.

Other stories are even more amazing. Doctors treated diabetic patients who were in comas. They were about to die. Soon after receiving insulin, these patients woke up, ate normal diets, and became strong again.

Right: *Elizabeth Hughes had a dramatic turn of health after she started taking insulin in the 1920s.*
Below: *Girls at a camp for diabetics learn how to monitor glucose levels and eat properly, as well as to give themselves insulin.*

HOW DO THEY *Know That?*

A diabetic who takes too little insulin will have too much glucose in his or her blood. Taking too much insulin will leave too little glucose. How do diabetics know how much insulin to take? First, they must figure out how much glucose is in the food they will eat. They can do this by reading labels on food packages and consulting nutritional charts. Then they inject the amount of insulin needed to move that amount of glucose into their cells *(below)*.

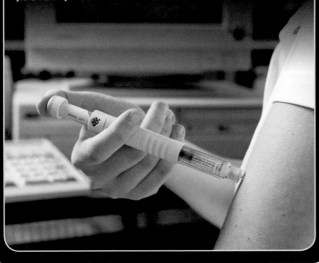

TWO TYPES OF DIABETES

Diabetes takes two forms: type 1 and type 2. Type 1 diabetes usually strikes children. It develops when a child's immune system damages his or her pancreas. Type 2 diabetes usually strikes adults. Doctors do not completely understand how type 2 diabetes develops. But they think that a poor diet, especially a diet high in sugar and white flour, puts people at risk for getting type 2 diabetes. Being overweight and not getting enough exercise also increase a person's chances of getting type 2 diabetes.

In the twenty-first century, many Americans are overweight. They have poor diets and do not get much exercise. As a result, more and more Americans are getting type 2 diabetes. To help prevent type 2 diabetes, it's important to eat protein, healthy fats (such as those found in nuts), and whole grains such as oats and brown rice. Daily exercise and keeping stress levels low help a lot too.

"Whoever has seen how a [diabetic] patient lying in agony soon recovers from certain death and is restored to actual health [by insulin] will never forget it."

—*German doctor Georg Ludwig Zulzer, 1923*

MODERN TREATMENTS

Doctors still treat many diabetics with insulin. But some type 2 diabetics don't need insulin shots. They can control their blood sugar just by following a good diet and exercising. In modern times, insulin does not come from animals. Instead, scientists use bacteria and yeast to make insulin in laboratories.

Many medical advancements have made diabetes easier to manage. In the twenty-first century, diabetics can check their own glucose levels with portable monitors. Some diabetics use insulin pumps that automatically inject insulin under their skin. With insulin pumps, people don't have to take shots several times a day. Diabetics can also choose types of insulin that work quickly and for a short time or work more slowly and for a longer time. These advancements help diabetics keep their glucose

WHERE DOES THE *Insulin Come From?*

Doctors can use insulin from many different animals to treat diabetes. The first insulin used to treat diabetes came from cows, pigs, and horses. During the 1940s, Japanese doctors used insulin from whales. Modern scientists make most insulin in labs. But a few drug companies still sell insulin from animals.

Modern companies make insulin in laboratories like the one pictured here.

Many diabetics use insulin pumps to monitor and control their diabetes. The pumps deliver insulin continuously and take the place of injections.

WHY ALL *the Shots?*

Many diabetics put insulin in their bodies by giving themselves shots. Why can't they just take pills to get insulin? Insulin is a substance called a protein. Acids and other substances inside a person's stomach break down proteins. If diabetics swallowed insulin in pill form, their stomachs would destroy the insulin before it could reach the bloodstream.

levels more stable. When glucose levels are stable, diabetics stay healthier.

Insulin treatments cannot keep blood sugar levels as stable as a normal pancreas can. Even with insulin, many diabetics become blind late in life. Others develop kidney disease or problems with blood circulation. Modern medical treatments can help diabetics avoid these problems.

With modern treatments, it is possible to live a long, full life with diabetes. Bret Michaels, the lead singer of the rock group Poison, was diagnosed with type 1 diabetes when he was six years old. He travels and performs all over the world. He just has to remember to take his insulin with him.

4 Antibiotics

This micrograph shows penicillin crystals. Penicillin was the first antibiotic discovered by scientists.

$\mathcal{I}$N EARLIER CENTURIES, MOST PEOPLE COULD NOT EXPECT TO LIVE TO OLD AGE. MANY BABIES DIED OF ILLNESS BECAUSE THEIR BODIES COULD NOT FIGHT GERMS WELL. EVEN SCHOOL-AGED KIDS GOT SICK WITH SERIOUS DISEASES AND SOMETIMES DIED. WOMEN OFTEN DIED SOON AFTER THEY HAD BABIES. BACTERIA CAUSED MANY OF THESE ILLNESSES.

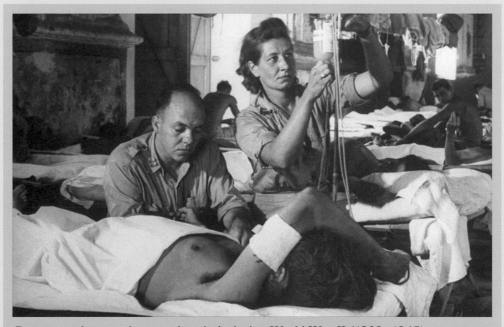

Doctors and nurses in army hospitals during World War II (1939–1945) were among the first to see the dramatic effects of antibiotics.

Many soldiers died during wars, and not just in battles. Germs spread through armies quickly. Bacteria grew in wounds. More soldiers died from illnesses and infections than from bullets.

Back then doctors could not cure illnesses caused by bacteria. They didn't know about medicines called antibiotics. Antibiotics are made by bacteria and funguses. These substances can kill or slow the growth of other organisms. The discovery of antibiotics changed the way doctors treated many diseases.

THE DISCOVERY OF PENICILLIN

Scientist Alexander Fleming worked at a university in Great Britain. On September 3, 1928, Fleming found a blue green mold growing in a dish with some bacteria that he was studying. He didn't want bacteria with mold. So he almost threw the dish away. Then he noticed something interesting. The mold made a brown substance that killed the bacteria growing near it.

Fleming realized that he was on to something. Could this brown substance—which he first called mold juice—be used to treat illnesses caused by bacteria?

Fleming named his mold juice penicillin. He found it could kill many

NOT *All* BAD

Bacteria are tiny one-celled creatures. They live all over the world. Some bacteria are dangerous. They are germs that cause disease. But most bacteria are harmless. Many are even helpful. Many kinds of bacteria help plants grow and help keep animals healthy. Other bacteria help the planet by turning dead plants and animals into soil. Some bacteria make antibiotics that doctors use to fight disease.

Alexander Fleming works in his laboratory in the early twentieth century.

PENICILLIN *in the Past*

The ancient Egyptians put moldy bread on wounds to help them heal. The Egyptians had no idea why the mold worked. They didn't know about germs. Modern scientists think that the mold on the bread was the same kind of mold that makes penicillin.

This mold culture is the same strain that Alexander Fleming found when he discovered penicillin in the 1920s.

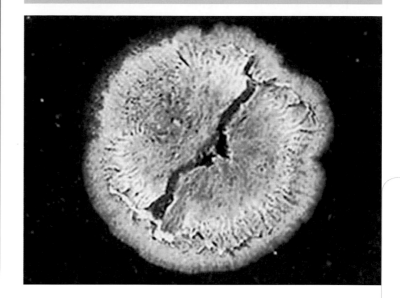

different disease-causing bacteria. He wrote articles about what he learned. He hoped to make lots of penicillin to test on sick people. He needed help from other scientists to do this. But they were busy with their own projects and weren't excited about penicillin.

THE DISCOVERY OF GRAMICIDIN

René Dubos, a French scientist, worked in the United States. He had grown up on a farm and had studied soil in college. Dubos thought of soil as a healing substance. He thought he might find medicine in the soil. In the 1930s, Dubos discovered bacteria in soil that made an antibiotic. He called the antibiotic gramicidin. This antibiotic could kill many disease-causing bacteria.

But gramicidin also destroyed red blood cells. So doctors couldn't inject it into patients' bloodstreams to cure diseases. Instead, doctors smeared it on

" [René Dubos] followed the supremely simple working hypothesis [theory] that soil as a self-purifying environment could supply an agent to destroy disease-causing bacteria."

—*Rollin D. Hotchkiss, who worked with Dubos, 1990*

wounds to protect patients from infections. Gramicidin saved many lives. But doctors knew they could save even more lives by injecting safer antibiotics into patients' bloodstreams.

MOLD JUICE TO THE RESCUE

An Australian scientist named Howard Florey read about Dubos's work. Florey worked in Great Britain with a German scientist named Ernst Chain. Florey and Chain also read Alexander Fleming's report about penicillin. They realized

Howard Florey (left) *and Ernst Chain* (below), *along with Alexander Fleming, won the 1945 Nobel Prize in Physiology or Medicine for their work with penicillin.*

PROTECTING *Penicillin*

During World War II, Howard Florey, Ernst Chain, and the rest of the team making penicillin worried about an enemy attack. The scientists knew that if the enemy German army invaded Great Britain, they would have to leave quickly. They needed a way to take penicillin with them. So the scientists spread a little bit of the mold inside their lab coats. If they had to leave quickly, they could use the mold on their coats to grow more.

that penicillin could be a lifesaving drug. With the help of other scientists, they began working with penicillin.

The scientists figured out how to get mold to make lots of penicillin. They made sure that penicillin could be given safely as a shot. Finally, they tested the penicillin to make sure it helped people who were sick. It worked very well.

By then World War II (1939–1945) had started in Europe. Doctors knew that penicillin could save soldiers' lives. It could also keep soldiers healthy so they could continue fighting. Scientists in Great Britain wanted to make a lot of penicillin very quickly. To do this, they needed large factories.

But British factories were busy making weapons and equipment for soldiers. They couldn't make much penicillin. Florey asked U.S. factories to help. Together, British and U.S. factories made lots of penicillin. They made enough to treat thousands of soldiers.

Doctors could give penicillin as a shot. So it was even better than gramicidin. Penicillin cured many sick soldiers and helped large wounds heal completely.

World War II ended in 1945. By then plenty of penicillin was available. It could treat many illnesses. Fleming's mold juice was a lifesaving drug.

"On this job you are creating a plant [factory] that will mean life and death to many men in the armed forces . . . the quicker our work is done, the quicker penicillin will be saving our fighting men."

—*note given to men building a factory to produce penicillin in the United States, 1943*

MORE ANTIBIOTICS

Doctors were excited about penicillin. It cured many sick people. But penicillin could not cure every illness. It could not cure tuberculosis, for instance. Tuberculosis, or TB, has made people sick for thousands of years. More than one billion people have died of TB. In earlier times, people with tuberculosis lived in special hospitals, where they would not infect other people.

Scientists searched for an antibiotic that could cure tuberculosis. Two of these scientists were Americans Albert Schatz and Selman Waksman. Schatz and Waksman looked for antibiotics the same way Dubos had done. They looked in soil and other places in nature. In October 1943, they found a fungus in a chicken's throat. The fungus made an antibiotic. Schatz and Waksman named

AGAINST *Life*

Antibiotics have saved many lives. But antibiotics aren't 100 percent safe. Antibiotics can't tell the difference between "good" bacteria and "bad" bacteria. So they kill some bacteria that our bodies need to stay healthy. This ability to kill bacteria—both good and bad—accounts for the name *antibiotics*. It means "against life." Some antibiotics can also damage a person's internal organs. Doctors must decide whether antibiotics are really necessary before prescribing them.

Child victims of tuberculosis pose for a picture at the Sea Breeze Hospital on Coney Island, New York, in the early twentieth century.

Above: *Selman Waksman was instrumental in discovering at least nine antibiotics in the 1940s. One of these, streptomycin, was the first antibiotic used to treat tuberculosis.* Below: *Modern antibiotics are usually taken in pill form.*

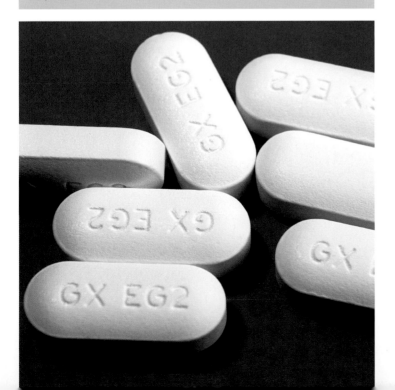

it streptomycin. They found that streptomycin killed many bacteria. It even killed the bacteria that cause tuberculosis.

Scientists tested streptomycin on animals. Then they tested it on people. They made sure it would cure tuberculosis and that it was safe. The antibiotic worked. Doctors finally had a way to treat tuberculosis.

MODERN ANTIBIOTICS

In the twenty-first century, doctors use antibiotics and other kinds of drugs to treat illnesses caused by bacteria. The doctors give antibiotics in pill form or as shots.

But we can't take antibiotics for granted. Some people take antibiotics every time they are sick. Sometimes, when people use too many antibiotics, bacteria develop ways to withstand the antibiotics. Then the antibiotics no longer work. So people should not take antibiotics unless they really need them.

Modern antibiotics can cure many illnesses caused by bacteria. Millions of people owe their lives to antibiotics. They are a powerful weapon against disease.

5 HEART *Transplants*

Doctors perform surgery in an operating room. Modern medicine makes heart transplants, once an unthinkable procedure, possible.

*A*FTER WORLD WAR II, DOCTORS COULD TREAT MANY SERIOUS ILLNESSES. BUT THEY COULD NOT HELP PEOPLE WHOSE MAJOR ORGANS DID NOT WORK WELL. MAJOR ORGANS INCLUDE THE HEART, LUNGS, KIDNEYS, AND LIVER.

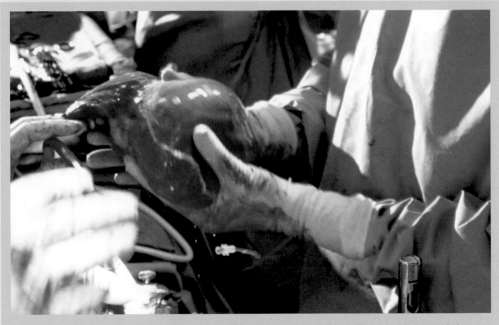

A surgeon holds a liver that he will transplant into a patient. Doctors began doing liver transplants in the 1960s.

Sometimes people are born with organs that do not work well. Other times, serious illnesses damage healthy organs. And some people do not take good care of their bodies, which hurts their organs. People die when their major organs stop working.

In modern times, doctors can replace many damaged organs with healthy organs from other people. The person who receives the organ is the recipient. The person who gives the organ is the donor. In most cases, organ donors have died, but some of their organs are still healthy enough to work in another person's body. In some cases, living people can donate organs or parts of organs.

REJECTION

Transplanting organs is difficult. Doctors practice for many years to do organ transplants. They learn how to take care of donated organs. Health-care workers must keep donated organs cold to protect them outside the body. They need to transport donated organs to recipients quickly. For example, doctors must transplant hearts and lungs within six hours of their removal from a donor.

One of the biggest problems for transplant surgeons is making sure that a recipient's body does not reject a donated organ. Tiny particles called molecules cover the cells in your body. Some of these molecules are unique to you. Your immune system recognizes the molecules that belong to you. But a recipient's immune system might not recognize the molecules in a donated organ. The immune system will attack that organ. This attack is called rejection.

THE FIRST
Transplants

Doctors performed transplants thousands of years ago. In ancient times, doctors transplanted skin from one part of the body to another. They used the skin to cover burns or wounds. In the early 1900s, surgeons transplanted corneas from one person to another. *(A modern cornea transplant is pictured below.)* Corneas are the clear coverings over the pupils in your eyes. Rejection is not a problem with skin and cornea transplants.

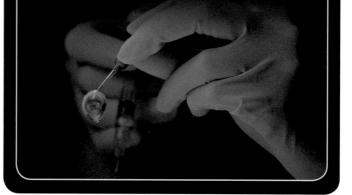

This response is normal. The immune system is supposed to protect the body from foreign things, such as germs. But rejection is a big problem in transplants. Rejection has killed many organ recipients.

To prevent rejection, doctors must make sure the molecules on the donor's cells are similar to the molecules on the recipient's cells. Before performing a transplant, doctors test blood samples from both donor and recipient to make sure the molecules are similar.

Close relatives usually have similar molecules on their cells. So the best organ donor is often related to the recipient. Relatives are especially useful in living donations. For instance, a living donor can provide a kidney, a lung, or part of a liver, pancreas, or intestine to a relative. But strangers can donate organs too.

Left: *A volunteer bone marrow donor gives a blood sample. Technicians will check the blood to see if it is a good match for the transplant recipient.* Right: *People can fill out organ donation cards so that family members and emergency workers will know they want to be donors.*

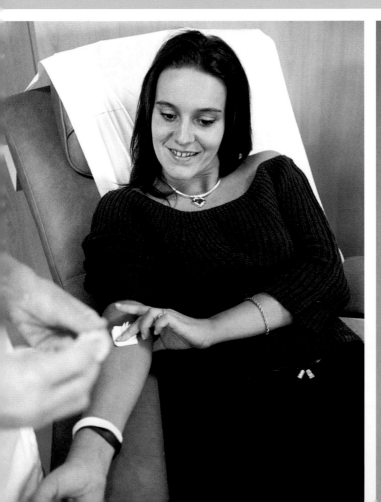

Donor Card
I would like to help someone to live after my death.

Let your relatives know your wishes, and keep this card with you at all times.

I request that after my death
*A. my *kidneys, *corneas, *heart, *lungs, *liver, *pancreas be used for transplantation, or
*B. any part of my body be used for the treatment of others
*(DELETE AS APPROPRIATE)

Signature_____ Date_____

Full name_____
(BLOCK CAPITALS)
In the event of my death, if possible contact:

Name_____ Tel._____

Even when the donor and recipient are a good match, the recipient's body will try to reject the donated organ. So doctors give recipients drugs that weaken their immune systems. A weakened immune system is less likely to attack a donor organ. Recipients have to take the drugs for the rest of their lives to protect the donor organs. But rejection sometimes happens even when recipients take the drugs.

The drugs also make recipients more likely to get sick. They get sick because their immune systems are too weak to fight germs.

After Demi Brennan (center, surrounded by two of her doctors) *received a new liver, her immune system changed. Unlike other transplant recipients, she does not need to take drugs to prevent rejection.*

DONATION *without* Rejection

An Australian girl named Demi Brennan received a liver transplant in the early 2000s. Several months after the operation, she no longer needed drugs to prevent rejection. She has stayed healthy and still doesn't need the drugs. Some cells of her immune system changed to become like the cells of the liver donor. The cells don't attack her new liver. Doctors are studying the girl to learn why her body changed. If they can find out, they might be able to change the cells in other transplant patients.

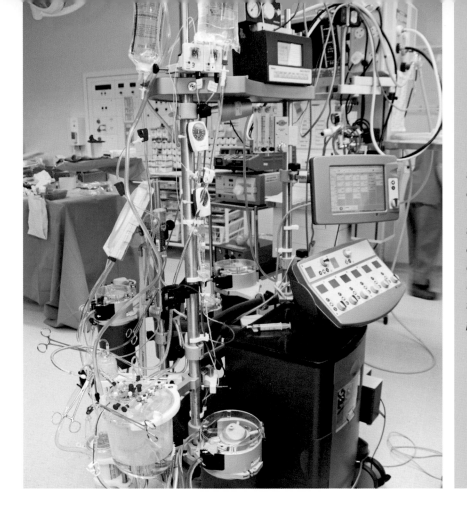

This heart-lung machine is ready to be used during surgery. Blood will pass through the machine, where carbon dioxide will be removed, oxygen added, and the blood reheated before it is pumped back into the patient's body.

STRAIGHT TO THE HEART

Kidneys are easier to transplant than other organs. Doctors figured out how to transplant kidneys in the 1950s. In 1963 doctors made the first successful liver transplant.

Transplanting a human heart proved to be the most difficult. In the 1950s, surgeons practiced by transplanting hearts from animal to animal. They got a big boost when scientists built a heart-lung machine in 1953. This machine took over the job of the heart and lungs during heart surgery. It enabled doctors to keep a patient's blood flowing without a heart.

With drugs to help prevent rejection, heart-lung machines to keep recipients alive during surgery, and many years of practice on animals, doctors were ready to transplant a human heart. But they faced one more problem. Many people did not like the idea of organ transplants. They didn't think doctors should take an organ from one body and put it into another. Science was moving faster than some people could accept.

Heart transplants caused even more worry. Some people thought that the heart contained the human soul. They believed a person who received a donor heart would also get that person's soul and personality. Doctors explained that the brain is the organ that controls personality. They said the heart is just a pump for blood.

CHIMP TO HUMAN

In 1964, at the University of Mississippi, Dr. James Hardy had a patient who badly needed a new heart. No human donor was available. So Hardy used a chimpanzee's heart. After Hardy transplanted the heart, it beat for ninety minutes. Then the patient died, simply because his body was so sick.

Hardy had taken a huge step in heart transplantation. But many people felt the operation was wrong. They said that human and animal body parts should not be mixed. Even other doctors said that Hardy should not have done it.

HUMAN TO HUMAN

Dr. Christiaan Barnard was a heart surgeon in South Africa. In 1967 he had a patient named Louis Washkansky. Washkansky was very ill. He needed a new heart.

Barnard found a brain-dead heart donor. A brain-dead person is someone whose brain no longer works, usually because the person was hurt in an accident. The person's brain does not work, but doctors can use machines to keep his or her lungs and heart working.

Barnard's team removed the donor heart while it was still beating. They transplanted it into Washkansky. For the first time, a heart that was formed in one person beat in the chest of another.

BECOMING A *Donor*

People who want to donate their organs after death can sign a special card or have a notice put on their driver's licenses. But if you want to donate your organs after death, the most important thing is letting family members know. If family members don't know one another's wishes, they might refuse to allow organs to be used for donation, even if someone has signed a donor card.

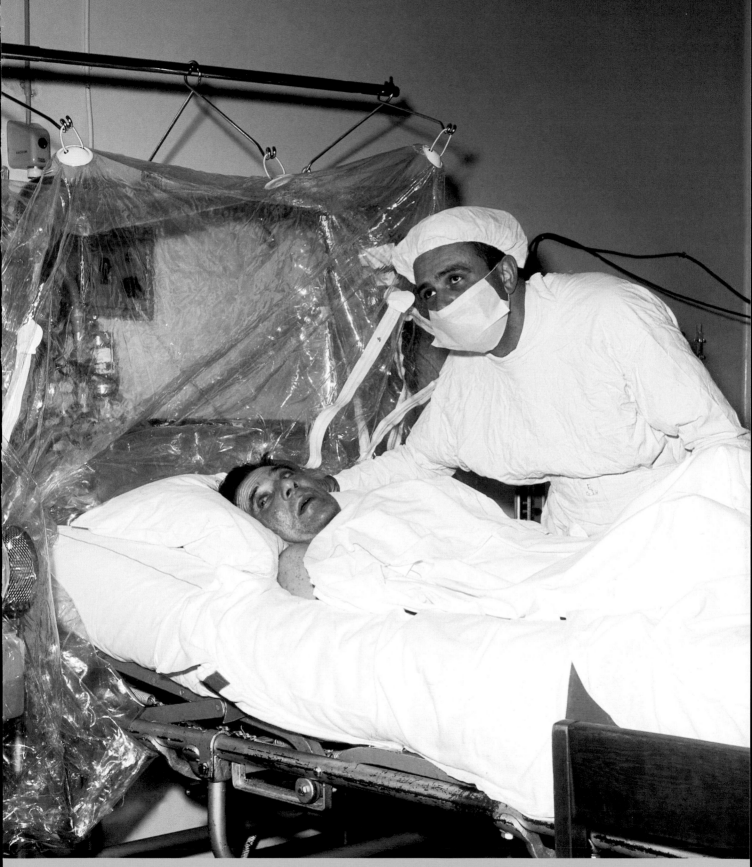

Dr. Chistiaan Barnard stands over the bed of Louis Washkansky after successfully performing the world's first heart transplant in 1967.

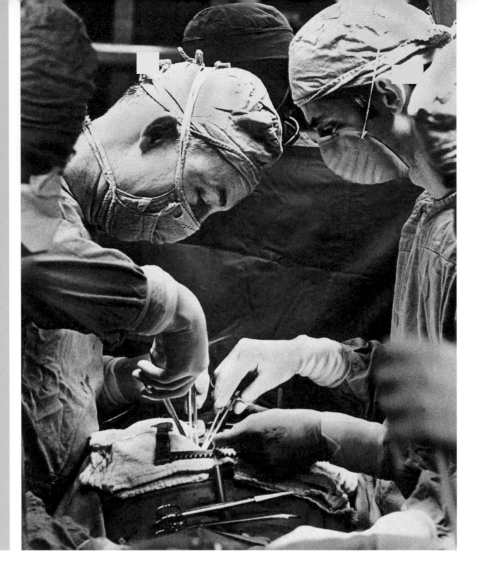

Dr. Norman Shumway performs a heart transplant on a patient in California in the late twentieth century.

Washkansky recovered quickly. The donor heart beat strongly. But then Washkansky caught pneumonia. He died just eighteen days after the operation.

Even though Washkansky died, the heart transplant had been successful. Americans became excited about the surgery. In the next two years, doctors in the United States performed more than one hundred heart transplants.

Many of these transplants were not successful. Many patients died of infection or rejection. Soon most heart surgeons stopped transplanting hearts.

"We have achieved a degree of experience with heart transplantation in the laboratory with which we feel confident we can take appropriate care of the patient with a cardiac [heart] transplant."

—*Dr. Norman Shumway, 1967*

"Even those for whom this extraordinary scientific feat was familiar were awed into silence as the heart, making itself at home, slowly began to pump."

—George Howe Colt, "Dylan's New Heart," 1990

THE BEAT Goes On

In the past, when doctors removed hearts from brain-dead donors, the hearts stopped beating. They started beating again after being transplanted. In 2006 doctors transplanted a beating human heart for the first time. Doctors removed the beating heart from the donor and placed it in a device called the Organ Care System. This machine kept the heart warm, beating, and fed with oxygen while it was transported to the recipient. Doctors have since used the system in many heart transplant operations. Recipients of beating hearts recover faster than people who receive hearts that have stopped beating and started again.

But Dr. Norman Shumway kept trying. He and his team worked hard to avoid organ rejection. Many of their transplantations were successful. This success showed other doctors that heart transplants could save lives.

In the twenty-first century, doctors around the world perform about four thousand heart transplants each year. Rejection is still a problem. But scientists keep improving drugs to prevent it. More than two-thirds of heart recipients live at least five years after the operation.

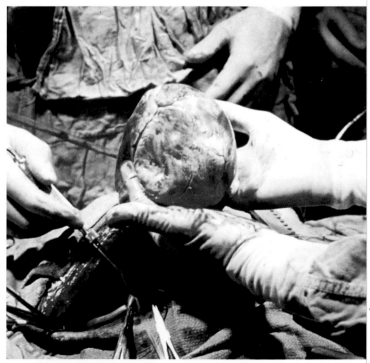

Surgeon Denton Arthur Cooley holds a heart just prior to implantation during a 1960s heart transplant.

6 The Human Genome Project

A researcher examines chromosomes as part of
the Human Genome Project. The computer screen
shows what he is seeing through the microscope.

SOME SERIOUS DISEASES, SUCH AS CYSTIC

FIBROSIS AND SOME KINDS OF CANCER, CANNOT BE CURED WITH

DRUGS OR SURGERY. THESE DISEASES ARE NOT CAUSED BY GERMS.

INSTEAD, THEY ORIGINATE INSIDE A PERSON'S GENES.

A scientist analyzes the chemical makeup of a gene.

Genes are material inside the cells of all living things, including plants and animals. Genes determine physical traits, such as eye color and hair color. Genes determine other traits too, such as blood type and intelligence. Parents pass on their genetic traits to their children. For instance, if both your parents have curly hair, your hair will probably be curly too. Parents can also pass on genetic diseases to their children. Diseases that pass from parents to children are called inheritable diseases.

FIRST STEPS

For thousands of years, doctors had no way to prevent or treat inheritable diseases. But in the 1800s, scientists began to study genes and how they pass from parents to children.

One of the first people to study genes was an Austrian scientist named Gregor Mendel. In the mid-1800s, he learned about genes by studying pea plants. Mendel crossbred a pea plant with smooth, round peas with another pea plant that had wrinkled peas. Each parent plant contributed genes to its offspring. One parent gave genes for round peas, and the other gave genes for wrinkled peas. But the offspring of the two plants all had round peas and no wrinkled peas.

Above: *Gregor Mendel paved the way for modern genetics.* Below: *This illustration shows what happened when Mendel bred yellow wrinkled peas* (top left) *with green round peas* (top right). *The first generation resulted in yellow round peas* (top center). *The second generation* (in pods) *had a mix of pea characteristics.*

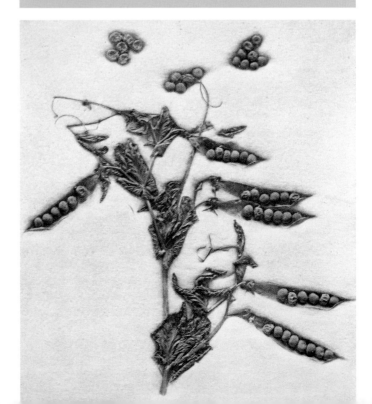

This experiment showed that the gene for round peas is dominant over the gene for wrinkled peas. This means that the gene for round peas masks, or covers, the gene for wrinkled peas. The gene for wrinkled peas is recessive, or hidden. The young pea plants had inherited the gene for wrinkles. But that trait was hidden in their cells. Mendel could produce pea plants with wrinkled peas only if both parent plants had the recessive gene.

THE STRUCTURE of DNA

Scientists James Watson and Francis Crick discovered the structure of DNA in 1953. DNA looks like a twisted ladder. The rungs of the ladder contain genetic information, the instructions that cells follow when they form, grow, and reproduce. The photo below shows Watson *(left)* and Crick with their model of the DNA molecule in 1953.

DNA CARRIES THE CODE

Mendel showed that offspring inherit genes from their parents. But he didn't know how. One hundred years after his experiments, scientists proved that genes are made of DNA.

The DNA in genes carries instructions for the formation, growth, and reproduction of living things. Cells can "read" and follow the instructions in genes. Each gene is a piece of DNA that carries instructions for a specific trait.

FROM PEAS TO PEOPLE

Just like Mendel's pea plants, people carry genes for different traits. These traits include some inheritable diseases.

Inheritable diseases result from a mistake in the DNA that makes up a gene. The mistake makes the gene faulty. Faulty genes give cells the wrong instructions to follow. Sometimes these wrong instructions cause diseases.

"Science has put a huge effort into explaining something people seem to understand at a very basic level: each child is like its parents."

—Jeremy Cherfas, science writer, 2002

One of these diseases is Huntington's disease. Huntington's disease affects the human nervous system—the network consisting of the brain, spinal cord, and nerves. The gene that causes the disease is dominant. If a person has just one gene for Huntington's disease, he or she will get the disease.

Cystic fibrosis is another inheritable disease. This deadly illness affects about seventy thousand people around the world. The disease causes a person's lungs to fill up with fluid. People with cystic fibrosis can die from their health problems.

The gene that causes cystic fibrosis is recessive. To get the disease, a person must inherit the gene from both parents. People who get the gene from only one parent do not get sick. But they are "healthy carriers" who can pass the gene on to their children.

THE HUMAN GENOME PROJECT

The network of all the DNA inside an organism is called its genome. All organisms, from the tiniest bacteria to the largest plants and animals, have genomes. The term *human genome* refers to the network of DNA inside a human being. No two people have exactly the same DNA, except for

CHROMOSOMES

Chromosomes *(below)* are tiny threadlike structures inside cells. Each chromosome contains many genes. Humans have twenty-three pairs of chromosomes in almost all their cells. Half the chromosomes (one of each pair) come from a person's mother, and half come from the father.

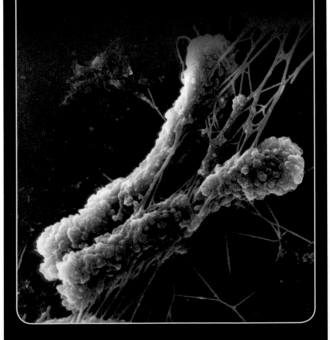

identical twins. But the human genome is basically the same for all people.

In the twentieth century, scientists wanted to learn more about the human genome. Understanding it would help them prevent and treat inheritable diseases. Scientists began the Human Genome Project in 1990. Their goal was to make a map of the human genome. The map would show all the genes in the genome. From the map, scientists could identify certain genes, such as genes that cause diseases. Identifying these genes would be the first step in curing the diseases.

A geneticist works on the Human Genome Project at the Whitehead Institute for Biomedical Research in Cambridge, Massachusetts, in the early 2000s.

FIRST PRIORITY

Since cystic fibrosis is such a deadly disease, scientists working on the Human Genome Project wanted to find that gene first. They found the gene in 1989, the year before the Human Genome Project officially began. After scientists found the gene that caused cystic fibrosis, they devised a test to show whether or not a healthy person carried the gene. People can take the test before they have children. If both parents carry the gene, they will know that their children might have cystic fibrosis.

Through the Human Genome Project, scientists have found that humans have 20,000 to 25,000 genes. Some of these genes cause many other inheritable diseases. One of these is a gene that leads to breast cancer. Some women, such as those whose mothers have had breast cancer, can take a test to see if they also carry the gene. If a woman learns that she has this gene, she can take precautions. She can examine her breasts more regularly and see her doctor often. If she does develop breast cancer, it will be found earlier. The earlier cancer is found, the easier it is to treat.

THE HOPE OF GENE THERAPY

The Human Genome Project involved scientists working in labs in many different countries. They first thought the project would take fifteen years. But because so many scientists cooperated, they finished the job earlier than expected. Scientists officially completed the project in April 2003.

The Human Genome Project has paved the way for new medical treatments. One of these treatments is gene therapy. It means to use DNA to treat diseases. With gene therapy, scientists might be able to create human genes in a laboratory. They could then replace faulty genes, such as the one

"The Human Genome Project (HGP) was one of the great feats of exploration in history—an inward voyage of discovery rather than an outward exploration of the planet or the cosmos [universe]."
—National Human Genome Research Institute, 2008

Scientists across the world, including these Chinese scientists, use information from the Human Genome Project to learn more about hereditary diseases.

that causes cystic fibrosis, with normal genes. But this work is not easy. And gene therapy might have dangerous side effects.

Scientists still have a lot of work to do to make gene therapy a reality. For instance, scientists have replaced the cystic fibrosis gene with a normal gene in tissue growing in a laboratory. But they have not yet been able to replace the cystic fibrosis gene with a normal gene in living animals. Scientists are working hard toward this goal.

Scientists hope to use gene therapy to cure genetic diseases. They hope to cure cystic fibrosis, many kinds of cancer, and many other diseases with gene therapy. If gene therapy is successful, many people's lives will be longer and healthier.

7 Nanomedicine

Richard Feynman (1918–1988) was the first scientist to talk about nanotechnology.

$\mathcal{M}$ODERN DOCTORS KNOW MORE ABOUT ILLNESSES AND HOW TO TREAT THEM THAN EVER BEFORE. GERMS STILL MAKE US SICK. BUT DOCTORS ARE ABLE TO TREAT AND CURE MANY DISEASES.

This researcher studies nanoparticles using an electron microscope.

Despite medical advances, people still have health problems. Doctors would like to make even more improvements in health care. For example, doctors would like to diagnose illnesses earlier. They can treat illnesses better when they find them early. Doctors would especially like to diagnose cancer earlier. Cancer kills one in five people in the United States. By finding cancer earlier, doctors could help more people survive the disease.

Doctors would also like to treat illnesses differently. The drugs used to treat many illnesses cause serious side effects. Chemotherapy drugs, which doctors use to treat cancer, are an example. In addition to fighting cancer, these strong drugs kill many healthy cells. The drugs can make cancer patients feel very sick.

Doctors would also like better ways to replace damaged body parts. Doctors sometimes replace damaged parts with artificial ones. For instance, doctors can replace defective hip joints with joints made from metal. But doctors would rather help the body repair its own tissue. Natural tissues are strong and work well with the rest of the body.

Doctors hope that a new kind of medicine, nanomedicine, will help them reach their goals for improved medical care. Nanomedicine involves using tiny tools to diagnose and treat diseases and injuries.

FEYNMAN'S DREAM

In 1959 a physics professor named Richard Feynman gave a talk to other scientists. His lecture was called "There's Plenty of Room at the Bottom." In it, Feynman described a new kind of science. This was a science of very small things.

In his lecture, Feynman asked physicists to invent better microscopes. The microscopes he envisioned would allow scientists to see the tiny protein and DNA molecules inside cells. Feynman also asked scientists to think about making tiny computers and other tiny machines. In 1959 Feynman's ideas seemed impossible. At that time, computers were so large that they filled entire rooms. How could a computer or other machine be made very small?

"What I want to talk about is the problem of manipulating and controlling things on a small scale."

—Richard P. Feynman, 1959

MEASURING IN *Nanometers*

One nanometer is one billionth of a meter. A DNA molecule is about 2 nanometers wide. Bacteria are about 1,000 nanometers wide. Red blood cells are about 7,000 nanometers wide. To get a sense of how tiny these measurements are, consider that a sheet of paper is about 100,000 nanometers thick.

Feynman's dream finally started to come true in the 1980s. In that decade, physicists invented very powerful microscopes like the ones Feynman had described. Scientists could use these microscopes to see atoms and to move them around.

The practice of moving and working with atoms and other tiny particles is called nanotechnology. The basic unit of measurement in nanotechnology is the nanometer. A nanometer is one-billionth the size of a meter (1 meter equals 3.3 feet). It takes 25 million nanometers to equal 1 inch (2.5 centimeters).

Nanotechnology has led to nanomedicine. So far, nanomedicine is still an experimental science. But one day, doctors hope to use it to diagnose and treat illnesses.

Scientists continue to invent more powerful microscopes, such as the protein microscope below, which allows scientists to view objects at resolution of 100 nanometers. Researchers believe this microscope will advance the treatment of a number of diseases.

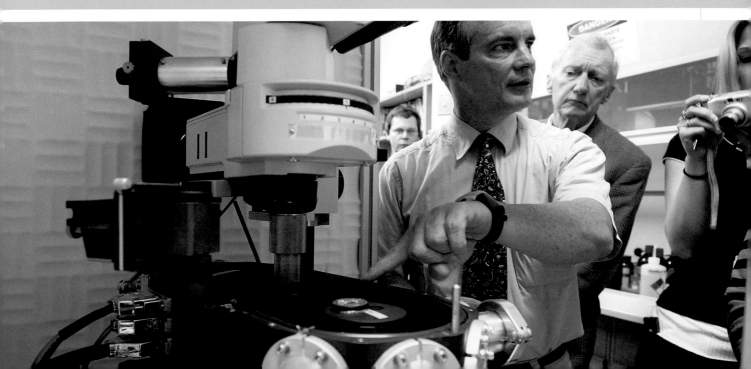

DIAGNOSIS

Doctors often check for illnesses using imaging technology, such as X-rays. Imaging tools allow doctors to see patients' bones, organs, and other body parts. A doctor might find a group of cancerous cells by looking at a lung X-ray, for example. But doctors would like to diagnose diseases such as cancer even earlier.

A nanotechnology called molecular imaging might allow doctors to find diseases much earlier. Molecular imaging will let doctors see tiny parts of the body, such as individual cells and molecules.

Here's how the process will work. A doctor will inject special proteins called probes into a patient's body. The probes will move through the patient's bloodstream until they reach diseased cells. They will then bind, or attach, to these cells. When the doctor shines a special light on the patient, the probes will start to glow. The doctor will watch the glowing cells on a monitor. In this way, the doctor will see the first signs of disease, before it spreads to more of the body. The doctor will then treat the disease right away, before the patient gets very sick.

LAB-ON-A-CHIP

Another nanomedicine device is the lab-on-a-chip. This chip is about the size of a dime. It has thousands of tiny wires. The tip of each wire contains a different probe. The probes stick to molecules from cancer cells or germs.

Here's how the lab-on-a-chip will work: A doctor will put a few drops of blood on the chip and then shine a special light on it. The probes will glow if the blood shows signs of disease.

The device is called a lab-on-a-chip because it will do tests that can normally be done only in a laboratory. Using a chip will be much faster and cheaper than running tests in a lab.

HOW DO THEY *Know That?*

How do doctors and scientists know that nanoparticles are safe for people? They don't know yet. Scientists also aren't sure whether the particles will hurt the environment when they are thrown away. Scientists must test nanoparticles. They must make sure they are safe for patients and for the environment before they use them.

SWALLOW THE *Doctor?*

Richard Feynman told scientists that one of his friends had an interesting idea. His friend wondered if one day a patient could "swallow the doctor." The friend envisioned tiny robot "doctors" traveling inside someone's body to fix it. Such "nanorobots" are still just a dream. But imagine the possibilities. What if tiny robots could go into cells and replace faulty genes with normal genes? What if they could destroy disease-causing germs without drugs? What if . . . ?

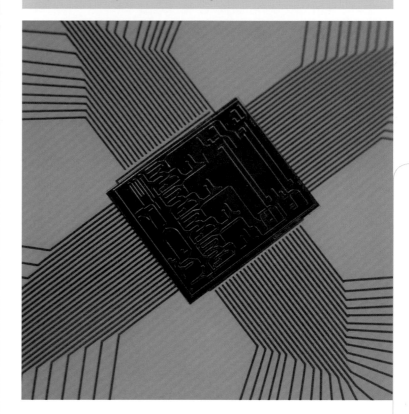

This image shows a prototype of a lab-on-a-chip, which is formally known as a microelectromechanical chip. Doctors hope to use chips like this to diagnose disease.

DRUG DELIVERY

Nanoparticles are particles that are 1 to 100 nanometers in size. Remember from page 63 that a sheet of paper is about 100,000 nanometers thick. Nanoparticles are small enough to travel through blood vessels. Scientists have many ideas about how to use nanoparticles in medicine. Here are just a few.

One day doctors might use nanoparticles to give vaccines. Modern doctors have to give patients the same vaccines several times. They give a first shot and later booster shots to make sure patients stay protected from a disease. In the future, doctors might inject patients with tiny gel capsules filled with vaccine nanoparticles. Once inside the body, the gel in the capsules will break down, releasing some of the vaccine. Later the capsules will release more vaccine. The patient will get all the vaccine he or she needs with just one shot.

One day nanoparticles might also help diabetics. Diabetics have to give themselves shots of insulin many times a day. The stomach destroys insulin, so diabetics can't swallow it in pill form. But scientists might put insulin inside nanoparticles that would protect the insulin in the stomach. The nanoparticles would release the insulin after it had left the stomach and moved to other parts of the body.

Nanomedicine might also be helpful in treating cancer. The most common treatments for cancer are risky. Strong cancer drugs and radiation treatments can have dangerous side effects. The treatments kill many healthy cells along with cancer cells. They make patients very sick.

Scientists might be able to cover nanoparticles with drugs and with molecules that will stick to cancerous tumors. The nanoparticles could travel through a patient's bloodstream, right to a tumor. The drugs could go to work right where they were needed. They would work better than other cancer treatments because they would pinpoint the cancer instead of spreading all over the body. The patient would have fewer side effects because fewer healthy cells would be damaged. Cancer treatments would be safer.

TISSUE REPAIR

Doctors might also use nanomedicine to treat damaged bones and other tissue. Patients sometimes need operations to fix broken bones. But one day, doctors might use carbon nanotubes instead. Nanotubes are long but very thin tubes made of carbon. They are strong and flexible.

Doctors will cover the nanotubes with molecules that attract the body's own bone-growing material. Doctors will then inject the nanotubes near the break in a bone. The body will build new bone on the nanotubes.

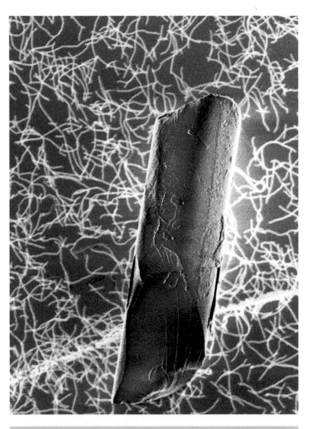

This image made with an electron microscope shows carbon nanotubes (in yellow). The tubes are much tinier than a human hair (purple).

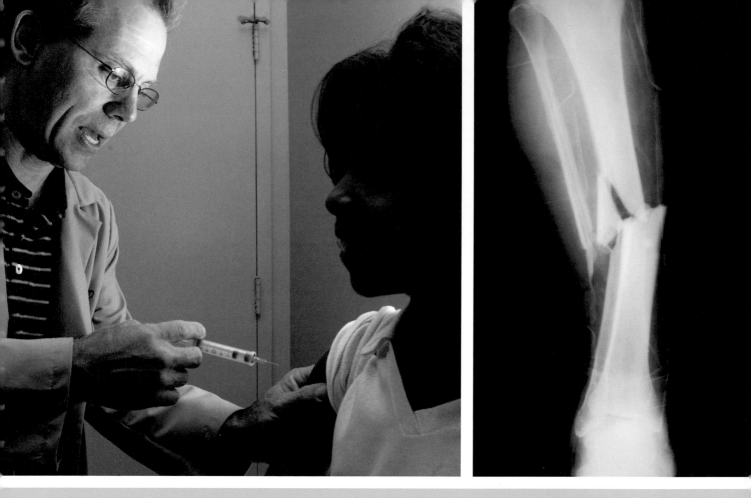

Doctors and researchers are searching for ways to use nanotechnology to change medicine. They hope to use nanotechnology to give vaccines (above left), *heal broken bones* (above right), *and treat cancer patients* (below).

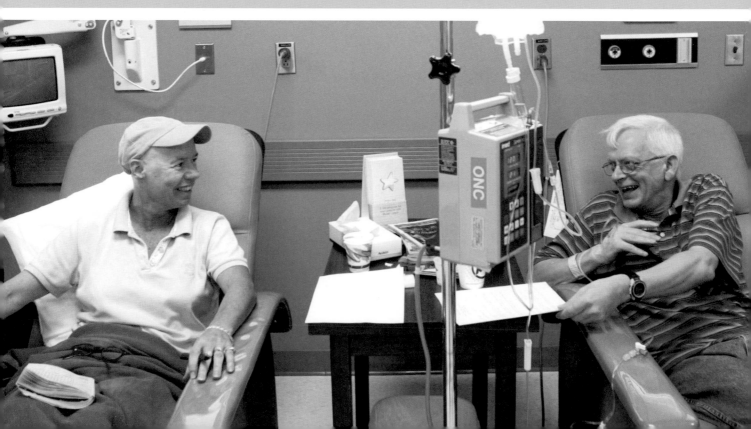

This computer illustration shows a carbon nanotube. Scientists want to use carbon nanotubes to help the body heal itself.

The new bone will grow and heal. In this way, nanotubes will help the body heal itself. This treatment might one day help people who need new knees and hips.

THE FUTURE IS NEAR

Scientists have successfully used nanomedicine in mice. In one experiment, scientists injected nanoparticles into mice with damaged hearts. After one month, their hearts worked almost as well as hearts in healthy mice. Scientists think the nanoparticles sent signals to nearby cells. Those cells caused new blood vessels to form. The new blood vessels healed the mice's hearts. Maybe one day, doctors will use this kind of treatment to help people who have had heart attacks.

In another experiment, scientists injected mice with nanoshells. Nanoshells are tiny glass balls covered with a very thin shell of gold. Scientists injected the nanoshells into mice with tumors. Once inside a mouse, the nanoshells traveled through its bloodstream to the tumor. A scientist then shined a special light on the mouse. The light made the nanoshells inside the mouse heat up. The heat from the nanoshells killed the tumor cells. The heat also killed a few healthy cells right next to the tumor, but not many. One day doctors might be able to use nanoshells to destroy tumors in humans.

Nanomedicine could make our lives longer and healthier. But doctors still have a lot of work to do before using it. They must test the new technologies to make sure they work in humans. After testing, doctors can use the technologies to treat patients. In the future, a trip to the doctor's office might be a very different experience.

"What we thought was impossible back in 1971 is a reality today. What we think is impossible today—a world in which no one would suffer or die from cancer—can become a reality if we make it happen together."
—Dr. Andrew von Eschenbach, National Cancer Institute, 2006

Timeline

ca. 1590   Two Dutch eyeglass makers create the first microscope.

1665   Robert Hooke publishes *Micrographia*.

1674   Antoni van Leeuwenhoek discovers bacteria.

1796   Edward Jenner creates the smallpox vaccine.

1850s–1860s   Gregor Mendel studies genetics.

1870s–1880s   Louis Pasteur creates vaccines for cholera, anthrax, and rabies.

1889   Oskar Minkowski and Joseph von Mering discover that the pancreas is involved in diabetes.

1921   Carl Nylen builds the first surgical microscope.

1922   Doctors first use insulin to treat diabetes.

1928   Alexander Fleming discovers penicillin.

1931   Ernst Ruska and Max Knoll build the first electron microscope.

1943   Albert Schatz and Selman Waksman discover streptomycin.

1953   Scientists build the first heart-lung machine. Scientists discover the structure of DNA.

1959   Richard Feynman presents his "There's Plenty of Room at the Bottom" lecture, launching discussion of nanotechnology.

1963   Doctors perform the first successful liver transplant.

1964   James Hardy transplants a chimpanzee heart into a human recipient.

1967   Christiaan Barnard performs the first human-to-human heart transplant.

1979   Smallpox is eliminated.

1981   Gerd Binnig and Heinrich Rohrer invent the scanning tunneling microscope.

1989   Scientists find the gene that causes cystic fibrosis.

1990   The Human Genome Project begins.

2003   Human Genome Project is completed. Naomi Halas invents nanoshells.

2006   Doctors transplant the first beating human heart.

2009   Scientists invent an "intelligent pill." It tells doctors where it is in the body.

Choose an Eighth Wonder

Now that you've read about the Seven Wonders of Medicine, do a little research to choose an eighth wonder. You may enjoy working with a friend.

To start your research, look at some of the websites and books listed on pages 75–77. (The more general titles, such as *Medicine*, will be most helpful.) Use the Internet and library books to look for more information. What other discoveries or inventions have been important in medicine? Think about inventions and discoveries that have

- *kept people from getting sick*
- *helped sick people get better*
- *made the lives of many people longer or more comfortable*

You might even try gathering photos and writing your own chapter on the eighth wonder.

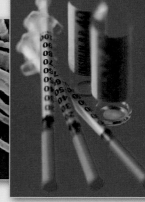

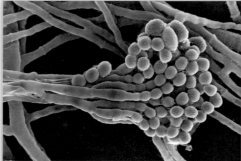

8

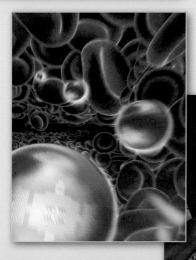

GLOSSARY AND PRONUNCIATION GUIDE

antibiotic (an-tih-by-AH-tihk): a substance made by bacteria and funguses that can kill or slow the growth of other organisms

antibody (AN-tih-bah-dee): a substance created by the immune system that helps the body fight germs

atom: the basic building block of matter

bacteria (bak-TIHR-ee-uh): simple, one-celled organisms. Some bacteria cause disease, while most are harmless.

cell: the basic unit of living things

chromosome (KROH-muh-sohm): a tiny threadlike structure inside cells. Chromosomes contain genes.

communicable disease: a disease that can be passed from one person to another

deoxyribonucleic (dee-AHK-sih-ry-boh-nu-klee-ihk) acid (DNA): genetic information that is passed from parent to offspring. DNA holds the instructions for the formation, growth, and reproduction of living things.

diabetes (dy-uh-BEE-teez): an illness that causes too much sugar to build up in a person's blood. Diabetes occurs when the body does not produce enough insulin or when the insulin cannot be used properly.

genes: material inside the cells of all living things that determines physical and other traits

genome (JEE-nohm): all the DNA in an organism

germ: a tiny living thing that causes disease

glucose (GLOO-kohz): a type of sugar the body uses to make energy

immune system: a network of cells and organs that fights germs

inheritable disease: a disease that can pass from parent to offspring

insulin (IHN-suh-luhn): a substance that helps glucose enter cells so that it can be used to make energy

magnify: to make objects appear larger

microscope: a device that uses one or more lenses to make things look bigger than they really are

molecular (muh-LEH-kyuh-luhr) imaging: technology that allows people to see individual cells and molecules

nanomedicine: nanotechnology used in medicine

nanotechnology: the practice of working with atoms and other tiny particles

organism: a living thing. Plants, animals, and bacteria are all organisms.

penicillin (peh-nuh-SIH-luhn): an antibiotic made by a certain type of mold

probes: substances that bind to certain molecules or cells

rejection: failure of a recipient's body to accept a donor organ. Rejection happens when the recipient's immune system attacks the new organ.

side effect: an unwanted result of a medical treatment

transplant: to move an organ or tissue from one part of the body to another or from one person (or animal) to another

vaccination (vak-suh-NAY-shuhn): an injection that protects animals from disease. Most vaccinations contain killed or weakened bacteria or viruses.

variolation (vuh-ree-uh-LAY-shun): using the smallpox virus to keep a person from getting smallpox naturally

virus: a tiny germ that can infect cells of animals and plants. Some viruses make people sick.

SOURCE NOTES

9   Victor Hugo, *Les Misérables* (Ware, UK: Wordsworth Editions, 1994), 606.

12 Howard Gest, *Microbes: An Invisible Universe* (Washington, DC: ASM Press, 2003), 5.

21 W. R. LeFanu, *A Bio-Bibliography of Edward Jenner* (London: Harvey and Blythe, 1951), 58.

23 World Health Organization, "Immunization," World Health Organization, 2009, http://www.who.int/topics/immunization/en/ (March 23, 2009).

29 Michael Bliss, *The Discovery of Insulin* (Chicago: University of Chicago Press, 1982), 152.

31 Ibid., 29.

37 C. L. Moberg and Z. A. Cohn, eds., *Launching the Antibiotic Era* (New York: Rockefeller University Press, 1990), 2–3.

39 K. Brown, *Penicillin Man: Alexander Fleming and the Antibiotic Revolution.* (Gloucestershire, UK: Sutton Publishing, 2004), 177.

50 Donald McRae, *Every Second Counts: The Race to Transplant the First Human Heart* (New York: G. P. Putnam's Sons, 2006), 23.

51 George Howe Colt, "Dylan's New Heart," *Life*, May 1990, 119.

56 Jeremy Cherfas, *The Human Genome: A Beginner's Guide to the Chemical Code of Life* (London: Dorling Kindersley, 2002), 6.

58 National Human Genome Institute, "All about the Human Genome Project (HGP)," genome.gov, 2008, http://www.genome.gov/10001772 (March 2, 2009).

62 Richard Feynman, "Plenty of Room at the Bottom," California Institute of Technology, 2009, http://www.its.caltech.edu/~feynman/plenty.html (March 22, 2009).

69 National Institutes of Health, "Working Together, We Can Defeat Cancer," *National Institutes of Health*, Summer 2006, http://www.nlm.nih.gov/medlineplus/magazine/issues/summer06/articles/summer06pg8-9.html (March 20, 2009).

SELECTED BIBLIOGRAPHY

Alper, J. "Chips Ahoy: The Lab-on-a-Chip Revolution Is Near." *NCI Alliance for Nanotechnology in Cancer*, April 2005, 1–3.

Behbehani, A. M. "The Smallpox Story: Life and Death of an Old Disease." *Microbiological Reviews* 47, no. 4 (1983): 455–509.

Bliss, Michael. *The Discovery of Insulin*. Chicago: University of Chicago Press, 1982.

Brown, K. *Penicillin Man: Alexander Fleming and the Antibiotic Revolution*. Gloucestershire, UK: Sutton Publishing, 2004.

Gest, Howard. *Microbes: An Invisible World*. Washington, DC: ASM Press, 1993.

Hardy, J. D. *The World of Surgery, 1945–1985*. Philadelphia: University of Pennsylvania Press, 1986.

Hopkins, D. R. *The Greatest Killer: Smallpox in History*. Chicago: University of Chicago Press, 1983.

Kriss, T. C., and V. M. Kriss. "History of the Operating Microscope: From Magnifying Glass to Microneurosurgery." *Neurosurgery* 42, no. 4 (1998): 899–908.

McRae, Donald. *Every Second Counts: The Race to Transplant the First Human Heart*. New York: G. P. Putnam's Sons, 2006.

Robbins, Jeffrey, ed. *The Pleasure of Finding Things Out: The Best Short Works of Richard P. Feynman*. Cambridge, MA: Perseus Books, 1999.

Tolstoi, L. G., and C. L. Smith. "Human Genome Project and Cystic Fibrosis: A Symbiotic Relationship." *Journal of the American Dietetic Association* 99 (1999): 1,421–1,427.

Williams, Linda, and Wade Adams. *Nanotechnology Demystified: A Self-Teaching Guide*. New York: McGraw-Hill Companies, 2007.

Zandonella, C. "The Tiny Toolkit." *Nature* 423 (2003): 10–12.

FURTHER READING AND WEBSITES

Books

Bailey, Gerry. *Medical Marvels.* London: Mercury Books, 2005. Bailey discusses many important achievements in medicine and explains how to make your own stethoscope, mechanical heart, and other medical devices. The book is cartoon illustrated.

Bankston, John. *Christiaan Barnard and the Story of the First Successful Heart Transplant.* Hockessin, DE: Mitchell Lane Publishers, 2003. Bankston describes how Christiaan Barnard, born into a poor family in Africa, came to be the first surgeon to transplant a human heart successfully. This achievement made Barnard famous and helped heart transplantation become an acceptable operation.

Brill, Marlene Targ. *Diabetes.* Minneapolis: Twenty-First Century Books, 2008. Brill explains the causes and symptoms of diabetes. She also describes treatment milestones, from the discovery of insulin to the most modern advancements.

Dowswell, Paul. *Medicine.* Chicago: Heinemann Library, 2002. Dowswell follows the invention of medical tools and procedures, including acupuncture, false teeth, and blood transfusions.

Fridell, Ron. *Decoding Life.* Minneapolis: Twenty-First Century Books, 2005. Learn how scientists have been working on unraveling the secrets of the genome and DNA.

Friedlander, Mark P., Jr. *Outbreak.* Minneapolis: Twenty-First Century Books, 2009. Friedlander explores epidemics that have affected much of the world, including outbreaks of smallpox, yellow fever, and bubonic plague. The book includes images of disease-causing organisms and explains how they harm their unwilling hosts.

Johnson, Rebecca. *Nanotechnology.* Minneapolis: Lerner Publications Company, 2006. Learn about the beginning of nanotechnology, how nanomaterials are made, and what the future holds.

Marrin, Albert. *Dr. Jenner and the Speckled Monster: The Discovery of the Smallpox Vaccine.* New York: Dutton Juvenile, 2002. This book gives the history of the smallpox virus, starting with its origins and tracing its spread around the world. The book also explains how Jenner's vaccine stopped smallpox epidemics.

Parker, Steve. *Medicine.* London: Dorling Kindersley, 2000. This heavily illustrated book explores the advancement of medicine from ancient to modern. Parker includes many of the discoveries and inventions that revolutionized medicine.

Silverstein, Alvin, Virginia Silverstein, and Laura Silverstein Nunn. *DNA.* Minneapolis: Twenty-First Century Books, 2009. This book explains what DNA is, how heredity works, what happens when DNA is miscopied, and how scientists have been learning to read the DNA code.

Woods, Michael, and Mary B. Woods. *The History of Medicine.* Minneapolis: Lerner Publications Company, 2006. In this detailed book, the Woodses examine great breakthroughs in the history of medicine, including vaccination and the discovery of antibiotics.

Yount, Lisa. *Antoni van Leeuwenhoek: First to See Microscopic Life*. Berkeley Heights, NJ: Enslow Publishers, 1996. This biography of Leeuwenhoek describes his work with microscopes and how it changed the world of science.

Websites

The Genomic Revolution

http://www.amnh.org/exhibitions/genomics/0_home/index.html
This website from the American Museum of Natural History explains how DNA was discovered, how genes work, what gene therapy means for us, and how DNA can be used to solve mysteries.

Infection, Detection, Protection

http://www.amnh.org/nationalcenter/infection/
This website from the American Museum of Natural History offers a colorful look at disease control.

KidsHealth

http://kidshealth.org/kid/
This website is designed just for kids. Learn how the body works, what causes different diseases, and how different kinds of doctors help people. This site has a dictionary of medical terms just for kids.

Nanooze

http://www.nanooze.org
Nanooze is a website about nanotechnology that was designed for kids. Learn about the basics of nanotechnology, as well as cool new inventions and techniques from the world of the very, very small.

INDEX

Adams, John, family, 18
animalcules, 10
anthrax, 12–13, 23
antibiotics: gramicidin, 37–38; modern uses, 41; penicillin, 34, 36–39; streptomycin, 40–41; tuberculosis, 40–41
antibodies, 17–18
atomic force microscopes, 15

bacteria: antibiotics and, 35–41; immunization from, 23; and microscopy, 12–14
Balmis, Francisco de, 20
Banting, Frederick, 28, 29
Barnard, Christiaan, 48–50
Best, Charles, 28, 29
Binnig, Gerd, 14
Brennan, Demi, 46

cancer, 53, 58, 59, 62, 64, 66
carbon nanotubes, 66–69
cells, 7, 10, 12, 13, 14; and genetics, 54–56; and nanotechnology, 62–66, 69; and organ rejection, 44–45, 46
Chain, Ernest, 38–39
cholera, 23
chromosomes, 56
Collip, James, 28, 29
communicable diseases, 7
concave lenses, 8
convex lenses, 8
Cooley, Arthur, 51
cornea transplants, 44
cowpox, 19–22
Crick, Francis, 55
cystic fibrosis, 53, 56, 58, 59

deoxyribonucleic acid (DNA), 13; and Human Genome Project, 55–58; and nanomedicine, 62, 63
diabetes, 24–33, 66
diagnosing, 64
diseases: and antibiotics, 35–41; hereditary, 53, 55–56, 58–59; microscopic detection of, 6, 12–13,

14; mystery of, 4–5, 7–8; nanomedical diagnosis of, 62, 64; vaccination against, 18–23
DNA. *See* deoxyribonucleic acid (DNA)
Dubos, René, 37–38

electron microscopes, 6, 14, 15
eyeglasses, 9

Feynman, Richard, 60, 62–63
Fleming, Alexander, 36–37, 38–39
Florey, Howard, 38–39
flu, 7

genes, 53–56
gene therapy, 58–59
germs, 12–13, 17, 35
glucose, 26, 30, 31
gramicidin, 37–38

Hardy, James, 48
heart-lung machines, 47
heart tranplants, 47–51
Hooke, Robert, 9–10, 11
Hughes, Elizabeth, 29–30
Human Genome Project: cystic fibrosis, 58; genes and DNA, 53–57; gene therapy, 58–59; origins, 56–57
Huntington's disease, 56

immune system, 17, 46
insulin: administering, 32–33; discovery, 26–29; effects of, 29–30; glucose monitoring, 30, 31; modern manufacturing, 32

Jenner, Edward, 16, 20

kidney transplants, 47
Knoll, Max, 14
Koch, Robert, 12–13

Leeuwenhoek, Antoni van, 10–12
light rays, 8

liver transplants, 46, 47

Macleod, John, 28, 29
measles, 23
medicine: history of, 4–5
Mendel, Gregor, 54–55
Mering, Joseph von, 26–27
Michaels, Bret, 33
Micrographia (Hooke), 10
microscopy: atomic force microscopes, 15; disease detection, 12–13, 14; early developments, 9–12; electron microscopes, 6, 14; lens strength, 8; and nanomedicine, 62–63; principle behind, 8; in surgery, 13
Middle Ages, 7, 9
Minkowski, Oskar, 26–27
molecules, 44
mumps, 23

nanomedicine, 61–62; diagnosis, 64–65; drug delivery, 65–66; future of, 69; and microscopy, 62–63; molecular imaging, 64; tissue repair, 66–69
Nylen, Carl, 13

organ donors, 48
organ transplants, 43–46

pancreas, 26–29
Pasteur, Louis, 22–23
penicillin, 34, 36–39
polio, 23

rabies, 23
rejection, tranplant, 44–45, 51
Rohrer, Heinrich, 14
Ruska, Ernst, 14

Salk, Jonas, 17
Schatz, Albert, 40–41
Shumway, Norman, 51
smallpox, 16, 18–22
Sotomayor, Sonia, 25
streptomycin, 40–41

ABOUT THE AUTHORS

Karen Gunnison Ballen has a bachelor's degree from Kalamazoo College in Kalamazoo, Michigan, and a doctoral degree from the University of Minnesota. She taught biology at a small college in Minnesota before turning to children's writing. She lives in Minnesota with her husband and children. *Seven Wonders of Medicine* is her first book.

PHOTO ACKNOWLEDGMENTS